Knox

by Iain Gray

79 Main Street, Newtongrange,
Midlothian EH22 4NA
Tel: 0131 344 0414
E-mail: info@lang-syne.co.uk
www.langsyneshop.co.uk

Design by Dorothy Meikle
Printed by Printwell Ltd
© Lang Syne Publishers Ltd 2024

All rights reserved. No part of this publication may be reproduced, stored or introduced into a retrieval system, or transmitted in any form or by any means (electronic, mechanical, photocopying, recording or otherwise) without the prior written permission of Lang Syne Publishers Ltd.

ISBN 978-1-85217-773-7

Knox

MOTTO:
I proceed and am more prosperous

CREST:
A dove

TERRITORIES:
Renfrewshire, Loch Lomondside

NAME VARIATIONS include:
Knock
Knocks
Nocks
Nox

Chapter one:

The origins of the clan system

by Rennie McOwan

The original Scottish clans of the Highlands and the great families of the Lowlands and Borders were gatherings of families, relatives, allies and neighbours for mutual protection against rivals or invaders.

Scotland experienced invasion from the Vikings, the Romans and English armies from the south. The Norman invasion of what is now England also had an influence on land-holding in Scotland. Some of these invaders stayed on and in time became 'Scottish'.

The word clan derives from the Gaelic language term 'clann', meaning children, and it was first used many centuries ago as communities were formed around tribal lands in glens and mountain fastnesses.

The format of clans changed over the centuries, but at its best the chief and his family held the land on behalf of all, like trustees, and the ordinary clansmen and women believed they had a blood relationship with the founder of their clan.

There were two way duties and obligations. An inadequate chief could be deposed and replaced by someone of greater ability.

Clan people had an immense pride in race. Their relationship with the chief was like adult children to a father and they had a real dignity.

The concept of clanship is very old and a more feudal notion of authority gradually crept in.

Pictland, for instance, was divided into seven principalities ruled by feudal leaders who were the strongest and most charismatic leaders of their particular groups.

By the sixth century the 'British' kingdoms of Strathclyde, Lothian and Celtic Dalriada (Argyll) had emerged and Scotland, as one nation, began to take shape in the time of King Kenneth MacAlpin.

Some chiefs claimed descent from ancient kings which may not have been accurate in every case.

By the twelfth and thirteenth centuries the clans and families were more strongly brought under the central control of Scottish monarchs.

Lands were awarded and administered more and more under royal favour, yet the power of the area clan chiefs was still very great.

The long wars to ensure Scotland's

independence against the expansionist ideas of English monarchs extended the influence of some clans and reduced the lands of others.

Those who supported Scotland's greatest king, Robert the Bruce, were awarded the territories of the families who had opposed his claim to the Scottish throne.

In the Scottish Borders country – the notorious Debatable Lands – the great families built up a ferocious reputation for providing warlike men accustomed to raiding into England and occasionally fighting one another.

Chiefs had the power to dispense justice and to confiscate lands and clan warfare produced a society where martial virtues – courage, hardiness, tenacity – were greatly admired.

Gradually the relationship between the clans and the Crown became strained as Scottish monarchs became more orientated to life in the Lowlands and, on occasion, towards England.

The Highland clans spoke a different language, Gaelic, whereas the language of Lowland Scotland and the court was Scots and in more modern times, English.

Highlanders dressed differently, had different

customs, and their wild mountain land sometimes seemed almost foreign to people living in the Lowlands.

It must be emphasised that Gaelic culture was very rich and story-telling, poetry, piping, the clarsach (harp) and other music all flourished and were greatly respected.

Highland culture was different from other parts of Scotland but it was not inferior or less sophisticated.

Central Government, whether in London or Edinburgh, sometimes saw the Gaelic clans as a challenge to their authority and some sent expeditions into the Highlands and west to crush the power of the Lords of the Isles.

Nevertheless, when the eighteenth century Jacobite Risings came along the cause of the Stuarts was mainly supported by Highland clans.

The word Jacobite comes from the Latin for James – Jacobus. The Jacobites wanted to restore the exiled Stuarts to the throne of Britain.

The monarchies of Scotland and England became one in 1603 when King James VI of Scotland (1st of England) gained the English throne after Queen Elizabeth died.

The Union of Parliaments of Scotland and England, the Treaty of Union, took place in 1707.

Some Highland clans, of course, and Lowland families opposed the Jacobites and supported the incoming Hanoverians.

After the Jacobite cause finally went down at Culloden in 1746 a kind of ethnic cleansing took place. The power of the chiefs was curtailed. Tartan and the pipes were banned in law.

Many emigrated, some because they wanted to, some because they were evicted by force. In addition, many Highlanders left for the cities of the south to seek work.

Many of the clan lands became home to sheep and deer shooting estates.

But the warlike traditions of the clans and the great Lowland and Border families lived on, with their descendants fighting bravely for freedom in two world wars.

Remember the men from whence you came, says the Gaelic proverb, and to that could be added the role of many heroic women.

The spirit of the clan, of having roots, whether Highland or Lowland, means much to thousands of people.

Meanwhile, many families proudly boast the heraldic device known as a Coat of Arms, as featured on our front cover.

The central motif of the Coat of Arms would originally have been what was sometimes borne on the shield of a warrior to distinguish himself from others on the battlefield.

Not featured on the Coat of Arms, but highlighted on page three, is the family motto and related crest – with the latter frequently different from the central motif.

Clan warfare produced a society where courage and tenacity were greatly admired

Chapter two:

Reforming zeal

In common with many names, 'Knox' and its spelling variants became popularised as a surname in the aftermath of the Norman Conquest of England in 1066 and subsequent spread of Anglo-Norman influence throughout the rest of the British Isles.

Previous to this, many people were identified in relation to a number of factors including where they lived, their occupation or physical characteristics.

As a locational name, 'Knox' derives from the Scots-Gaelic 'cnoc', or Old English 'cnocc', denoting 'hump', 'hillock 'or 'small, round-topped hill' – while one rather more colourful suggestion is that it was descriptive of a small, well-rounded, or stout man.

The consensus is that it is indeed a locational name, found as it is throughout Scotland and the north of England.

A family who adopted it as a surname are recorded at an early date as holding the barony of Renfrew, in present day Renfrewshire, and are said to have descended from 'Adam, son of Uchtred', who was granted lands at Knock at some point in the thirteenth century.

Further north from Renfrewshire, a William de (of) Knoc is recorded witnessing a transaction in relation to the 'Abbey of Lennox', in the Vale of Leven in 1273.

This transaction is of particular interest when we note that the Knoxes are considered a sept, or sub-branch, of Clan Macfarlane who, in turn, trace a descent from the Earls of Lennox whose heartland was the Vale of Leven.

Derived from the Gaelic *clanna*, meaning 'children', a clan was a close-knit tribal grouping settled in a particular territory and whose members – or 'children', or 'kin' – owed unswerving loyalty to a chief who was bound by duty and honour to protect them.

Not all members of a clan, such as the Knoxes, necessarily shared the same surname as the chief – known as *ceann-cinnidh*, meaning 'head and chief of the family' – and these 'kindred of the clan', or 'kinsfolk', were recognised, as they are to this day, as septs of the clan.

As such, they are entitled to share in its

heritage and traditions that include the right to display the clan tartan and heraldry of crest and motto – this recognised by the Lord Lyon King of Arms of Scotland, the final arbiter on all matters heraldic.

In the case of the Knoxes, they have their own proud motto 'I proceed and am more prosperous' and crest of a dove, but also share the Clan Macfarlane motto 'This I'll defend' and crest of a demi-savage wielding a sword and holding a crown.

As kinsfolk of the Macfarlanes, the Knoxes shared in not only their glorious fortunes but tragic misfortunes – and also, as we will find, in the fate of Mary, Queen of Scots.

Known in Gaelic as *Clann Pharlain*, the Macfarlanes boast a pedigree that stretches back through the dim mists of time to the Irish mythological Patholon, or 'Sea-Waves', said to have been the first to take possession of the Emerald Isle following the Flood.

With a descent from the earls, or Mormaers, of Lennox, whose territory in the present-day Vale of Leven embraced Loch Lomond, the Macfarlane heartland was the loch's western shore upwards of Tarbet.

In common with other clans, when not

battling external foes they found an outlet for their martial passions by preying on one another – in their case with their neighbours Clan Colquhoun.

So notorious were the Macfarlanes for their penchant of cattle-raiding by the light of the moon, that a full moon was wryly known in the locality as 'Macfarlane's Lantern.'

Acting for generations as light troops for the Earls of Lennox, one sixteenth century chronicler described them as 'light footmen, very well armed in the shirts of mail, with bows and two-handed swords.'

In the sixteenth century, the Macfarlane clan chief Andrew Macfarlane lent the support of his clansmen and kinsfolk such as the Knoxes to the body known as the Confederate Lords – who had forced Mary, Queen of Scots to abdicate in favour of her son, James VI (future James I of England).

On May 23, 1568, Mary's supporters, under the command of the Earl of Argyll, had been en route to the mighty bastion of Dumbarton Castle when they were intercepted near Glasgow by a numerically inferior but tactically superior force led by her half-brother the Regent James Stewart, 1st Earl of Moray.

Cannon fire had been exchanged before Argyll's infantry tried to force a passage through to the village of Langside, but they were fired on by a disciplined body of musketeers and forced to retreat as Moray launched a cavalry charge on their confused ranks.

The battle proved disastrous for Mary and signalled the death knell of her cause, with more than 100 of her supporters killed or captured and the queen forced to flee into what she then naively thought would be the protection of England's Queen Elizabeth.

But she was instead fated for confinement in

Mary, Queen of Scots

a succession of strongholds before her execution on February 8, 1587, in the Great Hall of Fotheringhay Castle, Northamptonshire.

Mary's defeat at the battle of Langside, meanwhile, would have been greeted with rejoicing by the fiery Protestant preacher John Knox, the main force in the religious revolution known as the Scottish Reformation, one of the most pivotal events in the nation's history.

Born in c.1514 in Haddington, East Lothian, the son of a merchant, this founder of the Presbyterian Church of Scotland is believed to have been educated at St Andrews University before working for a time as a notary priest, responsible for drawing up legal documents for the Catholic Church.

Disillusioned, however, he joined the ranks of the growing movement for religious reform and, in 1545, became the bodyguard of the charismatic preacher George Wishart.

In 1546, Wishart was tied to a stake and burned for heresy at St Andrews, while only a few weeks later Protestant sympathisers, who later took over the castle of St Andrews, assassinated Cardinal James Beaton, who had been instrumental in Wishart's brutal end.

Knox joined the rebels, but the castle was re-taken with the aid of a French force acting on behalf of Mary of Guise, who ruled Scotland in the name of her daughter, Mary, and Knox was exiled as a French galley slave, chained to the oars.

Released from servitude on the galleys at the beginning of 1549 and apparently none the worse of his ordeal, Knox arrived in England and then travelled north to take up a post as a preacher in Berwick and, after a subsequent spell of exile on the continent, returned to his native land in May of 1559.

A pen portrait of the religious zealot from this period describes him as being beneath average height, but with straight, well-proportioned limbs, and broad-shouldered.

Black-haired and with a swarthy complexion, he is also said to carry an air of natural dignity and authority, while his eyes are dark blue and animated, with his beard, flecked with grey, hung down 'a hand and half long.'

By the time this description was penned, the spark he had ignited by his impassioned preaching had fully fanned the flames of the Reformation across Scotland, consigning the old forms of worship to virtual oblivion.

In 1560 the Reformation was confirmed by the General Assembly of the Church and the Scottish Parliament, and was fully endorsed by both groups in December of 1567.

It was while he had been in exile that Knox wrote the infamous tract *The First Blast of the Trumpet against the Monstrous Regiment of Women*, published at Geneva in 1558.

It is a common misconception that this was a misogynistic attack on women, but Knox was far from being a hater of women – his second wife, whom he married in 1564, was the beautiful 16-year-old Margaret Stewart, daughter of Andrew Stewart, the 2nd Lord Ochiltree, of Ayrshire.

The 'regiment' of the title actually refers to the 'rule' of women, and was aimed in particular at Mary Tudor of England and Mary of Guise of Scotland.

On the rule of women, Knox had thundered that "to promote a woman to bear rule, superiority, dominion, or empire above any other realm, nation, or city, is repugnant to nature… and finally it is the subversion of good order, of all equity and justice."

This sentiment did not particularly endear him to the ill-starred Mary, Queen of Scots, when she returned from France to Scotland to take up her throne in 1561.

The preacher and his queen had heated discussions on four occasions when they met, Knox thundering at her in the style of an Old Testament prophet – while he was among those who later publicly called for her execution following the mysterious murder in 1567 of her husband the dissolute Lord Darnley.

Knox died in 1572, while rather ignominiously his body is believed to now lie beneath an Edinburgh car park.

His grim visage, however, looms over part of the landscape of Glasgow in the form of a statue atop a 58ft (17.78m) Doric column in the Glasgow Necropolis, to the east of Glasgow Cathedral.

Unveiled in September of 1825, thousands of spectators had lined the streets as the city's great and the good made their way in solemn procession to the necropolis – then a site known as Fir Hill until the necropolis was established seven years later.

The statue, fittingly, depicts the Father of the Scottish Reformation clad in clerical gown with his right arm half extended, the hand firmly clutching a Bible.

Chapter three:

Fame and infamy

One family of the Knox name has produced a dynasty of sons and daughters whose endeavours and pursuits range from the ecclesiastical sphere to literature and the arcane world of code-breaking.

Born in 1847 in Bangalore, India, Edmund Knox was the Bishop of Manchester who, through his mother Frances (née Reynolds), was a descendant of John Arbuthnott, 8th Viscount of Arthbuthnott, of Arbuthnott House, Kincardineshire and who died in 1860.

Following in his father's footsteps, Knox pursued a religious vocation, serving as 4th Bishop of Manchester from 1903 to 1921 and, before his death in 1937, becoming noted as an early proponent of cremation.

He had six children, one of whom, Alfred Dillwyn Knox, better known as Dilly Knox, was the classics scholar, expert on ancient parchments and code-breaker born in 1884.

Working as a code-breaker in the First World

War and, from 1939 until his death in 1943, at Bletchley Park code and cypher establishment in Buckinghamshire, he is portrayed by Richard Johnson in *Breaking the Code*, the 1996 television film about the top secret establishment.

One of his older brothers was Edmund George Valpy Knox, the satirist, author and editor of *Punch* magazine better known as E.V. Knox or by his pseudonym Evo.

Born in 1881 and editor of the magazine from 1932 to 1949, he died in 1971, while he was an older brother of the Catholic priest, theologian, author of detective stories and radio broadcaster Ronald Knox.

Born in 1888, one of his live broadcasts on the BBC, in January of 1926, caused a minor panic throughout the United Kingdom for a time.

Penned by Knox, his *Broadcasting from the Barricades*, 'reported' on a revolution that had broken out in London, with landmarks such as the Houses of Parliament destroyed by bombing and government ministers lynched by rampaging mobs.

Because it was broadcast over a particularly snowy weekend, it was not until some days later that newspaper deliveries throughout the country could return to normal – leading many people to believe their absence was, in fact, the result of a collapse in law and order.

A similar broadcast by Orson Welles from New York City in 1938, based on novelist H.G. Well's *The War of the Worlds*, also caused panic for a time – and Welles later credited Knox's broadcast as his inspiration.

He died in 1957, while he was a brother of the novelist and biographer Winifred Peck (née Knox), born in 1882.

The author of works including an acclaimed biography of Louis IX, she died in 1962, while she was the aunt of the award-winning biographer, poet and novelist Penelope Fitzgerald (née Knox).

Born in 1916 and the author of *The Knox Brothers* – a biography of her father E.V. Knox and her uncles and winner of the 1979 Booker Prize for her novel *Offshore* – she was the recipient one year before her death in 2000 of the Golden PEN Award by English PEN for a Lifetime's Distinguished Service to Literature.

One particularly infamous bearer of the Knox name was the Scottish anatomist and physician Robert Knox, implicated in the infamous early nineteenth century case of the Edinburgh 'body-snatchers' Burke and Hare.

Born in the city's North Richmond Street in 1791, he had a somewhat sinister appearance, having as a child contracted smallpox that destroyed his left eye and disfigured his face.

Passing the anatomy examination at Edinburgh University in 1814, he embarked on a career as an army medical officer, caring for wounded at the battle of Waterloo in June of 1815 and spending time in South Africa before being discharged in disgrace after falsely accusing a fellow officer of theft.

Undaunted, he returned to his native city to practise and teach anatomy at the university.

This was before the passing of the Anatomy Act of 1832, which made bodies available to anatomists, and the only

Dr Robert Knox

legal source of corpses for dissection were from felons who had been condemned by the courts to death and subsequent dissection.

But this 'supply' was never enough to meet the needs of the steadily growing number of medical students and anatomists such as Knox and, in common with others, he resorted to less legal means of acquiring bodies.

Such a supply became available in Edinburgh through William Burke and his partner in crime William Hare who, between 1827 and 1828 murdered at least sixteen of the city's poor and destitute and delivered their corpses – for a substantial fee – to Knox's dissecting rooms at Surgeons Square, now Surgeons' Hall.

Known as the West Port Murders, they caused a sensation when Burke and Hare were caught and put on trial in November of 1828.

Burke was hanged and faced the further ignominy of, ironically, having his body dissected and put on public display, while Hare, having turned King's evidence, escaped punishment.

Knox, the beneficiary of their gruesome and murderous spree, was not prosecuted – leading to widespread public outrage. His house was attacked by what a contemporary report described as 'the lowest rabble of the Old Town.'

No longer welcome in Edinburgh, Knox decamped to London where he worked in medical journalism and authored controversial articles on evolution and ethnology.

He died in 1862 and has since been the subject of a number of books and films that include the 1961 *The Anatomist*, portrayed by Alastair Sim and based on a 1930 play of the name by James Bridie.

Returning to the field of battle, and on American shores, David Knox was the photographer of the American Civil War of 1861 to 1865 born in one of the original Knox heartlands of Renfrew, in Scotland, in 1821.

Immigrating to America when aged 17 with his wife Elizabeth and his older brother John and his wife, he worked for a time as a machinist in Springfield, Illinois, for the Great Western Railroad.

Turning his talents to photography, he became an accredited photographer for the Union Army during the civil war, with some of his iconic shots – including one of a massive 13 inch mortar nicknamed 'Dictator' by the troops – included in *Gardners' Photographic Sketch Book of the War*; he died in 1937.

Chapter four:

On the world stage

An award-winning Canadian actor and novelist, Alexander Knox was born in 1907 in Strathroy, Ontario.

Working in England for a time in the 1930s and later starring on Broadway along with Jessica Tandy in a 1940 production of *Jupiter Laughs*, he came to wider attention for his role in the 1944 *Wilson*, a biographical film on American President Woodrow Wilson.

Produced by Darryl F. Zanuck, the film won Knox an Academy Award nomination for Best Actor and a Golden Globe Award – but during the 1950s he fell victim to the then anti-communist hysteria in the United States.

Although no communist, suspicion fell on him because of his liberal views and, in common with many others in his profession, he found a welcome refuge on British shores.

With film credits, in addition to *Wilson*, including the 1952 *Europa '51*, the 1958 *The Vikings* and the 1985 *Joshua Then and Now*, he was also a successful author of adventure tales including his 1971 *Night of the White Bear* and, from 1972, *The Enemy I Kill*.

Married to the actress Doris Nolan, with whom he had starred in his self-penned 1949 Broadway play *The Closing Door*, he died in 1995.

One of the longest serving cast members of the popular British television soap *Coronation Street*, **Barbara Knox** (nee Brothwood) is the actress born in 1933 in Oldham, Lancashire.

Making her stage debut at Oldham Coliseum Theatre in 1962, she first appeared in *Coronation Street* in the role of Rita Sullivan in 1964 for one episode, returning to the role full-time in 1972 and, in 2016, becoming the show's second-longest serving cast member after William (Bill) Roache, who has played the role of Ken Barlow since the first episode in 1960.

Winner of the 1989 *TV Times* Award for Best Actress and the 2004 British Soap Award for Lifetime Achievement, she is also the recipient of an MBE.

On American shores, Terry Davis is the actor of stage, film and television better known by his stage name **Terence Knox**.

Born in 1946 in Richland, Washington, his

television credits include, from 1982 to 1984, *St Elsewhere* and, from 1987 to 1990, *Tour of Duty*, while big screen credits include the 1992 *Children of the Corn II: The Final Sacrifice*.

Born in 1917 in Hartford, Connecticut, Elsie Lillian Kornbrath was the American actress and fashion designer better known by her stage name **Elyse Knox**.

Having initially embarked on a full-time career as a fashion model, modelling some of her own creations for *Vogue* magazine, she was talent-spotted by Hollywood and, in 1942, starred beside Lon Chaney, Jr., in *The Mummy's Tomb*.

A pin-up during the Second World War, frequently gracing the pages of the American forces' magazine *Yank*, she later found further fame as the character Ann Howe, sweetheart of the fictional boxer Joe Palooka in a series of *Joe Palooka* films based on the comic strip of the name; she died in 2012.

Beginning his acting career when aged 11 and appearing in television shows including *The Bill* and *Trust Me, I'm a Teenager*, Robert Knox, better known as **Rob Knox**, was the young English actor and murder victim born in 1989 in Bexley, London.

In 2008, after intervening in a fight to protect

his brother, he was stabbed outside a bar in Sidcup, in the southeast of London – his assailant, Karl Bishop, later sentenced to life imprisonment.

Before his death, he had acted in the role of Marcus Belby in the film *Harry Potter and the Half-Blood Prince* – appearing posthumously when it was released in 2009.

His legacy survives through the annual Rob Knox Film Festival, set up after his death by the Rob Knox Foundation to train young people in the arts.

Bearers of the Knox name have excelled in the highly competitive world of sport.

In the boxing ring, **Keith Knox**, born in Edinburgh in 1967, is the Scottish former professional boxer who held both the British and Commonwealth flyweight titles in 1999, while on the cricket pitch **Neville Knox** was a noted English batsman of the early1900s.

Born in 1884 in Clapham, London and having played for Surrey and recognised as one of the fastest bowlers ever to play for England – with speeds of more than 93mph (150km/h), he died in 1935.

On the golf course, **Russell Knox** is the Scottish professional golfer on the PGA (Professional Golfers Association) Tour who, born in Inverness in

1985, has had wins including the 2016 Travelers Championship.

From golf to football, **Archie Knox** is the Scottish former player born in 1947 in Tealing, Angus.

As a player his teams included Forfar Athletic, Dundee United and Montrose, while as a coach he has worked with Aberdeen, Manchester United, Rangers and Everton.

Notably, at Aberdeen as assistant manager to Alex Ferguson in the early 1980s, the team won two Scottish Cups, the European Cup Winners' Cup and the European Super Cup.

From sport to the creative world of art, **Simmie Lee Knox**, born in 1935 in Aliceville, Alabama, is the first Black-American to receive a presidential portrait commission.

Studying at Tyler School of Art, Pennsylvania, he first came to attention in the 1990s when commissioned by the entertainer Bill Cosby to paint twelve members of his family.

Also executing portraits of other famous figures including former boxer Muhammad Ali, he was commissioned in 2000 to paint the official portrait of President Bill Clinton and First Lady Hillary Clinton.

Back in the Knox homeland of Scotland, **John Knox** was the nineteenth century landscape artist born in 1778 and raised in Glasgow.

Known for selecting unusual spots to execute his paintings, such as atop mountains, his works include the c.1810 *Glasgow Green*, the c.1820 *The First Steamboat on the Clyde* and, from 1834, *South-Western View of Ben Lomond*; he died in 1845.

The main designer for a time of the Liberty Company, **Archibald Knox** was born in 1864 in Cronkbourne, Isle of Man – with his father from Kilbirnie, Ayrshire and mother from Lismore Island.

Embracing influences including Celtic Revival, Modernism, Art Nouveau and the Arts and Crafts Movement, most of his work for Liberty was in its pewter and precious metals ranges, including jewellery.

Particularly interested in Celtic art, which survives on his native Isle of Man in the form of ancient stone crosses, he died in 1933 while a set of stamps featuring his designs was released by the Isle of Man Post office in 2014.

In the music world, **Buddy Wayne Knox**, born in 1933 in Happy, Texas, was the American singer and songwriter best known for his 1957 hit *Party Doll*.

Elected to the Rockabilly Hall of Fame, he died in 1999, while *Party Doll* has been voted one of the Rock and Roll Hall of Fame's 500 Songs that Shaped Rock and Roll.

Bearers of the Knox name have also gained recognition in the world of science.

Born in 1927 and a professor of physical chemistry at Edinburgh University, **John Henderson Knox** is recognised as a pioneer in the fields of gas chromatography and reaction kinetics.

Developer of the Knox Equation relating to his fields of research, he died in 2018 while, as a keen yachtsman, he was also the inventor of the 'Anchorwatch' gauge which measures the force on an anchor chain.

In the world of the written word, William Knox, better known as **Bill Knox**, was the Scottish journalist, crime novelist and television broadcaster born in Glasgow in 1928.

Entering journalism when aged 16, he presented STV's *Crimedesk* series in the 1970s – becoming credited with popularising the term 'neds' to refer to young petty criminals.

Author of a number of crime novels, some under pseudonyms including 'Michael Kirk', he died in 1999.

One bearer of the Knox name with an unusual poetic legacy is the Scottish poet **William Knox**, the farmer's son born in 1789 in Lilliesleaf, Roxburghshire.

Author of a number of collections including his 1818 *The Lonely Hearth* and, from 1825, *Harps of Zion*, he died in 1825 – after having latterly led a rather dissolute life and which, one source rather disapprovingly observes, included entering the journalistic profession.

But the poet and erstwhile journalist is remembered for his poem *Mortality* – the favourite poem of American President Abraham Lincoln and which he could recite from memory.

The last verse reads:

> *From the blossom of*
> *health to the paleness*
> *of death,*
> *From the gilded saloon*
> *To the bier and the*
> *shroud –*
> *O why should the spirit*
> *Of mortal be proud!*